My First Acrostic

Little Poets From The South

Edited by Jonathan Fisher

First published in Great Britain in 2010 by:

Young Writers
Remus House
Coltsfoot Drive
Peterborough
PE2 9JX
Telephone: 01733 890066
Website: www.youngwriters.co.uk

All Rights Reserved
© Copyright Contributors 2010
SB ISBN 978-1-84924-875-4

Foreword

The 'My First Acrostic' collection was developed by Young Writers specifically for Key Stage 1 children. The poetic form is simple, fun and gives the young poet a guideline to shape their ideas, yet at the same time leaves room for their imagination and creativity to begin to blossom.

Due to the young age of the entrants we have enjoyed rewarding their effort by including as many of the poems as possible. Our hope is that seeing their work in print will encourage the children to grow and develop their writing skills to become our poets of tomorrow.

Young Writers has been publishing children's poetry for over 19 years. Our aim is to nurture creativity in our children and young adults, to give them an interest in poetry and an outlet to express themselves. This latest collection will act as a milestone for the young poets and one that will be enjoyable to revisit again and again.

Contents

Tilly Lomax (6) 1

Ardeley St Lawrence CE (VA) Prmary School, Ardeley
Lottie Weller (6) 2
Tommy Iontton Le Bonn (6) 3
Christopher Shaw (7) 4
Rex Thomson (7) 5
Caspar Bowley (5) 6

Arthur Dye Primary School, Cheltenham
Ryan Curran (6) 7
Lara Williams (6) 8
Aiden Smith (6) 9
Millie Didcote (6) 10
Olivia King (6) 11
Paris Perkins (6) 12

Burford Primary School, Burford
Niemi Craig (6) 13
Ella Swann (7) 14
Tiffany Mackie (6) 15
Amy Buckland (5) 16
Edward Proctor (5) 17
Bethany Timms (6) 18
Samuel Blantz (5) 19
Patrick Bowl (6) 20
Stella Atim-Kenlock (6) 21
Orlando Nelson (6) 22
Sophie Rawlings (7) 23
Ethan Learoyd (5) 24
Kirsty Locke (5) 25

Courtney Primary School, Kingswood
Joe Foxhall (6) 26
Chloe Nicholls-White (6) 27
Jodie Jefferies (7) 28
Jason Hobbs (6) 29
Nicolé Lesauteur (6) 30
Holly Derrick (6) 31
Joshua Elliott (7) 32
Aidan Box (6) 33

Luis Tucanovici (6) 34
Cameron Watson (6) 35
Freya de la Mare (6) 36
Jaiden Bracey (6) 37
Kesheba Evans (6) 38

Cranborne Primary School, Potters Bar
Charli O'Connor (6) 39
Joseph Yianni (6) 40
Archie Bett (6) 41
Aaron Smith (6) 42
Kira Crawshaw (6) 43
Oliver Miller (7) 44
Liam Stacey (6) 45
Lydia Rhodes (6) 46
Oliver Allison (6) 47
William Mellenfield (7) 48
Josh Mead (6) 49
Max Branch (6) 50
Zainab Syed (6) 51
Olivia Davies (6) 52
Mia Brennen (6) 53
Abbie Mole (6) 54
Janita Ross (6) 55
Scott Willard (6) 56
Tom Bateman (6) 57
James Allison (6) 58
Max Russell (6) 59
Sofia Burnham (6) 60
Jamie Crew (6) 61
Tommy Niblett (6) 62
Farhan Qurashi (6) 63
Ellie Batchelor (6) 64
Rebecca Turney (6) 65
Fern Kemp (6) 66
Matthew Herron (6) 67
Sophie Johnson (6) 68
Cain James (6) 69

Duncombe School, Bengeo
Lewis Head (6) 70
Alice-May Goddard (6) 71

Lauren Parsons (6) 72
Ben Halligan (6) 73
Libby Mae Sullivan (7) 74
Yasmin Jenkins (6) 75

Ellwood Primary School, Ellwood

Harry Sillence (7) 76
Hayden Edey (7) 77
Jack Watkins (7) 78
Chelsea Willetts (6) 79
Ella Powles (7) 80
Leon Broom (6) 81
Toni Tyler (6) 82

Finstock CE Primary School, Finstock

Cerys Louise Ireland (6) 83
Jack Millard (6) 84
Barney Foot (6) 85
Max (6) 86
Lizzy Jones (6) 87
Lucinda South (6) 88
Lexi Tipton (6) 89
Lily Holifield, Seth Keats-Hodkinson (6)
& Rosie Mullins (5) 90
Harriet Howard (5) 91
Megan Williams (6) 92

Green Lanes Primary School, Hatfield

Felicity Marshall (5) 93
Aliya Nawaz (5) 94
Iffat Ahmed (6) 95
Katie Jeffrey (5) 96
Mia Greenham (6) 97
Hannah Paget (5) 98
Michael Camm (5) 99
Matthew Perkins (6) 100
Harry Dobson (6) 101
Tyana Lister (6) 102
Katrina Smith (6) 103
Luke Mann (5) 104
Chloe James (6) 105
Haylan Dunham (6) 106
Alfie Raynsford (5) 107
Holly Toms (6) 108

Harry Ballard (5) 109
Ruby Hollywood-Martin (5) 110
Katie Coan (6) 111
Benjamin King (6) 112
Tayla Swaffield (6) 113
Patrick James Obcena (6) 114
Matthew Agathangelou (6) 115
Abbie Cook (6) 116
Molly Hoy (6) 117
Callum Gowing (6) 118
Sophia Monchar (6) 119
Zuhayr Mukuddem (6) 120
Joshua Long (6) 121
Zoe Hunter (6) 122
Lucian Antippa (7) 123
Flower Rosario (6) 124
Reece Van Genderen (6) 125
Dana Van Genderen (6) 126
Erin Reyner (6) 127
Missie Salmon (6) 128
Zainab Jeppe (6) 129
Liam Benson (6) 130
Joshua Paul (7) 131
James Mann (6) 132
Eve Betteridge (6) 133
Gemma Cutbill (5) 134

Howe Dell Primary School, Hatfield

Katie Leefarr (6) 135
Freddie Houlahan (6) 136
Shaun Michael Shoda (6) 137
Jodie Garg (6) 138
Bailey Quinn (6) 139
Stephanie Raine (6) 140
Harry-Tom Brinkley (6) 141
Ayo Ajayi (6) 142
Emma Roberts (6) 143
Tanvi Sofat (6) 144
Sophia Kleovoulou (6) 145
Kiera Chapman (6) 146
Scarlett Brown (6) 147
Camryn Whitney (6) 148
Georgia Stratton (6) 149
Mia Ross (7) 150
Trystan Sam-Fat (6) 151

Longcot & Fernham Primary School, Longcot
Rene Burke (6) 152
Katie Griffin (5) 153
Max Whitfield (7) 154

Maple Cross JMI & Nursery School, Maple Cross
Daisy Harvey (6).............................. 155
Charlotte Hatswell (6) 156
Bradley Holloway (6) 157

Meldreth Primary School, Meldreth
Alexandra Maggs (6) 158
Amelia Close (6) 159
Aoife Brophy (6) 160
Conall Fergus (6) 161
Elisha Plester (6) 162
Erin Fergus (6) 163
Leila Kermani (6) 164
Morgan Robson (6) 165
Shannon Casling (6) 166
Tia Misgrove (6) 167

Minchinhampton Primary School, Minchinhampton
Joshua Sibley (7) 168
Grace Southgate (6) 169
Jenny Weir (6) 170
Holly Rebecca Hamblin (6) 171
Ronan Lynch (6) 172

St Hilda's School, Harpenden
Amy Miller (6).................................... 173
Becky Walter (6)............................... 174
Tilly Johnstone (6)............................ 175
Madeline Pritchard (6) 176
Lottie Bentall (6) 177
Annabel Davis (6) 178
Eve Graham (6)................................ 179
Maddie Desmond (6) 180
Charlotte Gibson (6) 181
Hannah Ritchie (6) 182
Ella Murphy (6).................................. 183
Rosaleen Mackie (6) 184

Sibford Junior School, Sibford Ferris
Matthew Kinnersley (6)..................... 185
Elena Swift (5) 186
Oliver Meadows (6) 187
Sam Jervis (5) 188
Sammy Vintcent (5) 189

Trotts Hill Primary School, Stevenage
Connor Lightfoot 190
Kieran Lawrence (6) 191
Zoe Booyse (6) 192
Brandon Cowen (6) 193
Hannah Field (6) 194
Darcée Norton (7) 195
Siân Yvonne Worton (6).................... 196
Caitlin Hood (6) 197
Bilal Ahmed (7).................................. 198
Quincy Hayward Provencal (7) 199
Megan Wilkins (6).............................. 200
Gemma Hemmings (5)..................... 201
Shane Clynes (5) 202
Alex McCarthy (5) 203
Kimberley Glander (5) 204
Rebecca Honeysett (5) 205
Alicia Bachelor (5) 206
Caitlin Redmond (5).......................... 207
Abigail Craig (5) 208
Charlie Andrews (5) 209
Charlie Cameron (5) 210
Olivia O'Sullivan (5) 211
Pembe Pekoz (5) 212
Jack Mitchell (5) 213
Oliver Crake (5)................................. 214
George Ashby (5) 215
Reece Sullivan (5)............................. 216
Huan Xu (5) 217
Leo Ferrari (5).................................... 218
Cameron King (5).............................. 219
Oliver Wright (6) 220

Wheatcroft Primary School, Hertford
Jodie (5)... 221
Elise Ainge (5) 222
Chloe Carter (6) 223

Lara Craig (6) 224
Alastair Murray (7) 225
Rebecca Collins (6) 226
Elizabeth Appleford (6) 227
Kieran Paxton (6) 228
Sophie Pratt (6) 229
Leanna Rhodes (6) 230
Toby Hill (6) 231
Hester Peart (5) 232
James Welch (5) 233

The Poems

My First Acrostic – Little Poets From The South

My Poem

T illy is kind
I like the smell of roses
L ips are red
L ists are very good
Y o-yos are her favourite

L ight is very bright
O ffices
M ostly her pet moves
A eroplanes
eX citing foxes are very sneaky.

Tilly Lomax (6)

Lottie

L ipstick I like putting on
O range is my favourite colour
T umble often
T icklish often
I nnocent
E xcellent at literacy.

Lottie Weller (6)
Ardeley St Lawrence CE (VA) Primary School, Ardeley

Science Boy

T error Tommy

O range

M arvellous at science

M aker of models

Y ellow chips I love to eat.

Tommy Iontton Le Bonn (6)
Ardeley St Lawrence CE (VA) Primary School, Ardeley

Acrostic Boy

C ool at skateboarding
H appy because I had friends
R eading is good
I llustrator of books
S afe boy
T idying lullaby
O range is my favourite colour
P eaceful I am
H elpful to sad people
E xcited at literacy
R unning good at.

Christopher Shaw (7)
Ardeley St Lawrence CE (VA) Primary School, Ardeley

Maths Boy Rex

R ed is my favourite colour
E xcellent at maths
X -rayed once, it is fun!

Rex Thomson (7)
Ardeley St Lawrence CE (VA) Primary School, Ardeley

Caspar The Horseman

C lever at science
A musing at riding
S trong as a knight
P erfect at jumping
A te my dinner
R ed T-shirts are my favourite coloured clothes.

Caspar Bowley (5)
Ardeley St Lawrence CE (VA) Primary School, Ardeley

My First Acrostic - Little Poets From The South

Ryan

R yan wears red all the time
Y oung and nice
A little king
N ice to everyone.

Ryan Curran (6)
Arthur Dye Primary School, Cheltenham

Lara

L ovely Lara and happy Lara
A nice Lara and good Lara
R eally kind and caring Lara
A pretty girl Lara.

Lara Williams (6)
Arthur Dye Primary School, Cheltenham

My First Acrostic - Little Poets From The South

Aiden

A iden is nice and kind
I am six years old
D o you like blue and red?
E xcited Aiden
N ice, kind and friendly.

Aiden Smith (6)
Arthur Dye Primary School, Cheltenham

Millie

M illie has got blue eyes
I nteresting Millie
L ovely Millie
L ovely, extremely kind Millie
I n a happy mood Millie
E xcited Millie.

Millie Didcote (6)
Arthur Dye Primary School, Cheltenham

Olivia

O livia is beautiful and perfect
L ovely and colourful
I 'm beautiful but I do not have earrings
V ery colourful house
I 'm extremely beautiful
A m a queen and I'm shiny.

Olivia King (6)
Arthur Dye Primary School, Cheltenham

Paris

P aris is a princess
A lways dressing up
R iding my bike
I n my house I'm tidy
S tamping my feet.

Paris Perkins (6)
Arthur Dye Primary School, Cheltenham

My First Acrostic - Little Poets From The South

Niemi

N ibbling chocolate is nice
I am happy and sad
E njoy school
M onkeys eat bananas
I like going to the park.

Niemi Craig (6)
Burford Primary School, Burford

Ella Swann

E ggs are excellent
L ollipops are nice
L oops and more loops
A nna is my little sister

S weets are nice
W onderful big me
A ngel is me
N uts are nice
N ice is me.

Ella Swann (7)
Burford Primary School, Burford

My First Acrostic – Little Poets From The South

Tiffany

T V is my second favourite
I ce is nice in a drink of juice and Coke
F unny is my third favourite
F unny at home
A pples are my favourite fruit
N ice and kind to everybody
Y o-yos are my favourite out of toys.

Tiffany Mackie (6)
Burford Primary School, Burford

Amy

A pples are sweet
M onkeys are naughty
Y oghurt is yummy.

Amy Buckland (5)
Burford Primary School, Burford

Edward

E lmer is an elephant
D ucks are swimming
W orms are wiggly
A nts are crawling on the door
R hinoceroses are fighting
D ogs are chasing cats.

Edward Proctor (5)
Burford Primary School, Burford

Bethany

B eautiful Bethany
E ggs are tasty
T ea is good to drink
H ot chocolate is yummy
A pples are yummy
N early seven as well
Y oghurts, yummy, yummy in my tum.

Bethany Timms (6)
Burford Primary School, Burford

My First Acrostic - Little Poets From The South

Sam Blantz

S wimming in the deep end is fun
A pples are yummy
M agic is something I like doing

B ouncing on a trampoline
L ike my Hot Wheels track
A lways trying to win
N aughty Sam
T V is something I like
Z ebras in Madagascar are cool.

Samuel Blantz (5)
Burford Primary School, Burford

Patrick Bowl

P lay Lego
A nd lessons
T rees grow apples
R at
I like apples
C amp
K wik cricket

B owling
O ranges
W ill I be good?
L unch is important.

Patrick Bowl (6)
Burford Primary School, Burford

My First Acrostic – Little Poets From The South

Stella Atim-Kenlock

S weets and school
T V and stereos
E lephants and jelly
L aughs a lot
L ikes making things
A pples and cars and books

A nimals
T oys
I ce cream and Cornwall's great
M y sister Michelle
-
K icking a football is fun
E ggs are nice
N ever touch my chicken's eye
L ollies
O n a trampoline I jump high
C ake and pets I like
K irsty is my friend.

Stella Atim-Kenlock (6)
Burford Primary School, Burford

Orlando

- **O** ranges
- **R** ides at the fair
- **L** eaf collecting
- **A** lways playing on my PlayStation
- **N** ice friends
- **D** og, Jaffa
- **O** ver the wall.

Orlando Nelson (6)
Burford Primary School, Burford

My First Acrostic – Little Poets From The South

Sophie Rawlings

S weet girl my daddy said
O ur family has love
P laying with my friends is fun
H umming songs is graceful
I like school
E venings are tiring

R unning is fun
A breather would be good to stop running
W eeping when I am sad
L icking lollipops
I love my cats
N anas and grandmas I like to hug
G oing to birthday parties
S miling is what I do best.

Sophie Rawlings (7)
Burford Primary School, Burford

Ethan

E ggs are nice scrambled
T aps give you water
H oney is runny
A pples are sweet
N ice playing roly-poly.

Ethan Learoyd (5)
Burford Primary School, Burford

My First Acrostic - Little Poets From The South

Kirsty

K icking balls
I like cats
R unning
S weets
T iny babies
Y ellow.

Kirsty Locke (5)
Burford Primary School, Burford

Autumn

A nimals start to hibernate
U mbrellas blow inside out
T ree's leaves fall off
U mbrellas blow all ways
M ud is squishy
N ature changing.

Joe Foxhall (6)
Courtney Primary School, Kingswood

My First Acrostic - Little Poets From The South

Autumn

A nimals start to hibernate
U mbrellas get really wet
T rees are really colourful
U mbrellas go inside out
M ud is really mucky
N ature is changing.

Chloe Nicholls-White (6)
Courtney Primary School, Kingswood

Autumn

A nimals sleeping
U mbrellas blowing
T rees change colour
U nderground animals hibernate
M ud is squishy
N ature is changing.

Jodie Jefferies (7)
Courtney Primary School, Kingswood

My First Acrostic - Little Poets From The South

Autumn

A nimals are safe in holes in the ground
U p in the sky the birds are cold
T he changing colours, the leaves are beautiful
U p in the sky there's wind
M ud is mucky and squishy
N ature is changing brown.

Jason Hobbs (6)
Courtney Primary School, Kingswood

Autumn

A nimals sleeping
U mbrellas blow inside out
T rees are beautiful
U p in the sky are fireworks banging
M ud is damp and gooey
N uts being taken by squirrels.

Nicolé Lesauteur (6)
Courtney Primary School, Kingswood

My First Acrostic - Little Poets From The South

Autumn

A nut
U mbrella
T rees
U nderground animals
M ice sleep
N uts.

Holly Derrick (6)
Courtney Primary School, Kingswood

Autumn

A nimals start to hibernate
U mbrellas get wet
T he birds fly to hot countries
U mbrellas got windy
M e and Freya pick up conkers
N uts fall off the trees.

Joshua Elliott (7)
Courtney Primary School, Kingswood

My First Acrostic - Little Poets From The South

Autumn

A nimals start to hibernate
U mbrellas are good because they are waterproof
T he birds fly to hot countries
U p in the sky there are clouds and birds flying
M ud is gooey and people get muddy
N ature is changing and people like it.

Aidan Box (6)
Courtney Primary School, Kingswood

Autumn

A nimals start to hibernate
U mbrellas go inside out
T rees' leaves fall off
U mbrellas are waterproof
M ud is damp and mucky
N uts get taken by squirrels.

Luis Tucanovici (6)
Courtney Primary School, Kingswood

My First Acrostic – Little Poets From The South

Autumn

A corns
U mbrellas
T rees
U nderground animals
M ice sleep
N uts are stocked up.

Cameron Watson (6)
Courtney Primary School, Kingswood

Autumn

A pples are red
U mbrellas keep the wind from your hair
T wigs on the floor
U p in the sky, autumn is everywhere
M ud is slimy and sticky
N uts like conkers are fun.

Freya de la Mare (6)
Courtney Primary School, Kingswood

My First Acrostic - Little Poets From The South

Autumn

A rat is sleeping in a hole
U mbrellas blowing in the wind
T he leaves fall off the trees
U p in the sky the birds fly
M ud is soggy
N o sunshine until summer.

Jaiden Bracey (6)
Courtney Primary School, Kingswood

Autumn

A nts get the leaves ready

U mbrellas are good for the rain

T ia always shares her conkers with me

U p in the sky rain

M ud is everywhere

N uts and conkers are changing and fall.

Kesheba Evans (6)
Courtney Primary School, Kingswood

My First Acrostic - Little Poets From The South

Charli

C ake is my favourite food
H appy people make me happy
A ctivities I like include football and tennis
R unning rascal I am
L ucky Charli is my nickname
I nterested in football.

Charli O'Connor (6)
Cranborne Primary School, Potters Bar

Joseph

J oseph loves the rain
O n my bag I have a car
S ister's name is Hosanna
E xcellent at drawing
P laying with my friend
H ungry I am all the time.

Joseph Yianni (6)
Cranborne Primary School, Potters Bar

My First Acrostic – Little Poets From The South

Archie

A lways listens
R ugby is my favourite sport
C oke is my favourite drink
H arry is my pet goldfish
I like playing games
E at lots of chocolate.

Archie Bett (6)
Cranborne Primary School, Potters Bar

Aaron

A nts are my favourite bug
A lways sensible
R ed is my best colour
O ctober, I like Hallowe'en
N othing scares me.

Aaron Smith (6)
Cranborne Primary School, Potters Bar

My First Acrostic - Little Poets From The South

Kira

K ind and very excited about school
I like Lydia
R uns as fast as a leopard
A kind girl who really wants to learn.

Kira Crawshaw (6)
Cranborne Primary School, Potters Bar

Oliver M

O n September the 14th I am eight
L azy every Sunday
I like pizza
V ideo games I think are great
E ating lots of sweets
R unning is my favourite sport.

Oliver Miller (7)
Cranborne Primary School, Potters Bar

My First Acrostic - Little Poets From The South

Liam

L oves playing football
I like finding insects in the leaves
A lways laughing
M y favourite food is chicken casserole.

Liam Stacey (6)
Cranborne Primary School, Potters Bar

Lydia

L ovely as a friend
Y ellow hair
D elicate with people
I like my birthday party
A bsolutely determined to learn.

Lydia Rhodes (6)
Cranborne Primary School, Potters Bar

My First Acrostic – Little Poets From The South

Oliver

O range is my favourite colour
L ikes football
I ce hockey is a sport that I enjoy doing
V ery good at drawing
E xcellent at tennis
R ugby is my favourite

A wesome
L ike baseball
L ie in bed all day
I nterested in bugs
S uper at reading
O llie likes lollies
N ovember, I like fireworks.

Oliver Allison (6)
Cranborne Primary School, Potters Bar

William

W illiam likes whales
I 'm determined to get a handwriting pen
L eader of my ghost club
L azy in the morning
I nterested in ghosts
A nimals are fascinating
M ighty and strong.

William Mellenfield (7)
Cranborne Primary School, Potters Bar

My First Acrostic - Little Poets From The South

Josh

J osh likes running
O range is my favourite fruit
S un is my favourite weather
H elpful at school.

Josh Mead (6)
Cranborne Primary School, Potters Bar

Max

M y hair is brown
A lways playing
X cellent at swimming.

Max Branch (6)
Cranborne Primary School, Potters Bar

My First Acrostic - Little Poets From The South

Zainab

Z ainab likes zebras
A lways plays nicely with her sister
I s a good friend
N ever grumpy
A fraid of crocodiles
B irthday is in March.

Zainab Syed (6)
Cranborne Primary School, Potters Bar

Olivia Davies

O livia likes olives
L isten to the teachers
I like to eat sweets
V acuum cleaner tidies things away
I like to eat
A big hairy spider crawled up my back

D addy went to work early in the morning
A ll the birds wake up in the morning
V ery good Olivia
I like to run
E ggs come from birds
S ee the blackbirds.

Olivia Davies (6)
Cranborne Primary School, Potters Bar

My First Acrostic – Little Poets From The South

Mia Brennen

M ean Mia
I n school
A nd dirty

B rilliant at reading
R unning gets me tired
E xcellent Mia
N ever late to school
N ever late to dinner
E ven good at swimming
N ever bad.

Mia Brennen (6)
Cranborne Primary School, Potters Bar

Abbie

A bbie likes dogs and cats
B ikes are fun
B ikes are fantastic
I 'm very good on a bike
E ggs are yummy.

Abbie Mole (6)
Cranborne Primary School, Potters Bar

My First Acrostic - Little Poets From The South

Janita Ross

J anita
A nd Mia
N ever are bad
I like Mia
T ommy likes Mia
A nd now it is raining

R unning makes me exhausted
O ctopus is an animal I don't like
S lithery
S nakes live in the jungle.

Janita Ross (6)
Cranborne Primary School, Potters Bar

Scott Willard

S wimming Scott
C artwheeling Scott
O dd Scott
T ired Scott
T ennis Scott

W obbly Scott
I nteresting Scott
L end a hand Scott
L azy Scott
A ble to walk Scott
R unning race Scott
D aft at home Scott.

Scott Willard (6)
Cranborne Primary School, Potters Bar

My First Acrostic – Little Poets From The South

Tom

T umble Tom
O ctopus Tom
M onster Tom

B atman Tom
A lligator Tom
T elevision Tom
E lephant Tom
M onkey Tom
A nt Tom
N ice Tom.

Tom Bateman (6)
Cranborne Primary School, Potters Bar

James Allison

J ames jumps
A nd Scott jumps
M ake James invisible
E xcellent James
S ings to Scott

A t home I
L ive
L ovely
I n a
S cary
O rchard and
N ever eat apples.

James Allison (6)
Cranborne Primary School, Potters Bar

My First Acrostic – Little Poets From The South

Max Russell

M ax likes football
A n
X -ray machine

R un
U p the hills
S am likes football
S am likes playing with me
E than is good
L ike baseball
L ots of sweets.

Max Russell (6)
Cranborne Primary School, Potters Bar

Sofia

S ofia is good at sums
O livia is my friend
F amily takes care of you
I like literacy
A lessia is nice

B urnt toast for my breakfast, yuck
U p I went in a paraglider
R unning up high
N etting the fish
H appy birthday Sofia
A bbie is my friend
M ia is my very best friend.

Sofia Burnham (6)
Cranborne Primary School, Potters Bar

My First Acrostic - Little Poets From The South

Jamie

J amie likes eating jelly
A lways likes playing
M y mum is really nice
I like eating
E ach and every day.

Jamie Crew (6)
Cranborne Primary School, Potters Bar

Tommy

T ommy likes Lego
O ctopus Tommy
M onster Tommy
M ighty Tommy
Y awning Tommy

N ice Tommy
I ncredible Tommy
B urning Tommy
L oved Tommy
E ntertaining Tommy
T ricky Tommy
T idy Tommy.

Tommy Niblett (6)
Cranborne Primary School, Potters Bar

My First Acrostic - Little Poets From The South

Farhan

F arhan likes football
A t matches he scores goals
R eally good at tackling
H e really likes his football trainers
A t tackling he is good
N ight, I sometimes play football.

Farhan Qurashi (6)
Cranborne Primary School, Potters Bar

Ellie

E llie likes to play
L ovely safe lays in bed
L ots of smiles
I f it snows she plays snowballs
E llie likes school.

Ellie Batchelor (6)
Cranborne Primary School, Potters Bar

My First Acrostic - Little Poets From The South

Rebecca Turney

R ebecca is funny
E gg is yummy to me
B ed is my favourite place
E very day I play with Oscar
C hurches are my favourite things
C urry is my favourite food
A nnie May is my friend

T easing is naughty
U g is a rude word to me
R unning is my favourite thing
N othing
E lephants are my favourite animals
Y eah!

Rebecca Turney (6)
Cranborne Primary School, Potters Bar

Fern

F ern likes frogs
E leanor is my friend
R usset apples are my favourite
N ice people are good to me.

Fern Kemp (6)
Cranborne Primary School, Potters Bar

Matthew

M atthew is mental
A nimals I like
T urtles are my favourite animal
T homas is my brother
H erron is my surname
E lephants are a great sight to see
W ater is my favourite thing.

Matthew Herron (6)
Cranborne Primary School, Potters Bar

Sophie Johnson

S ophie is silly
O ranges are my favourite
P eas are my favourite vegetable
H exagons are my favourite shape
I like my teddy bear
E ating is my favourite thing to do

J ogging is my favourite sport
O oglies is my favourite programme
H ens are my favourite animal
N othing scares me
S ophie likes books
O bstacle races are my favourite
N estals is my pet fish.

Sophie Johnson (6)
Cranborne Primary School, Potters Bar

My First Acrostic – Little Poets From The South

Cain James

C ain is good at school
A t home I'm good
I t is good when I watch a film
N o, I'm not putting my toys away

J ames is happy at home
A t home I have a lovely bedroom
M y dad eats toast
E ating is fun
S un is what I like to look at.

Cain James (6)
Cranborne Primary School, Potters Bar

Batman

B atman he's dressed in black
A ll the baddies he's on their track
T he Joker and his evil pack
M ake a plan to steal a stack
A nd Batman is always on their back
N ow knocks them down with a crack.

Lewis Head (6)
Duncombe School, Bengeo

My First Acrostic – Little Poets From The South

Heroes!

C atwoman is a super villainess
A dored by Batman
T he Catwoman is Selina Kyle

W ears and carries a whip
O ne scary lady
M ean and frightening
A ctive and nimble
N ot to be trusted.

Alice-May Goddard (6)
Duncombe School, Bengeo

Super People

B atman can climb walls
A nd has a bat motorbike
T he Bat Motorbike lives in a bush
M ighty powers
A nd indestructible
N othing can stop him.

Lauren Parsons (6)
Duncombe School, Bengeo

My First Acrostic - Little Poets From The South

Heroes

B aby in a red costume
A nd strong and powerful
B aby Incredible wears a red mask
Y es, he is good

I ncredibles are secret, nobody knows who they actually are
N ot scared of danger
C lever and strong
R eally amazing
E xcellent at saving people's lives
D oesn't worry about danger
I nvincible and incredible
B est at fighting villains
L oves playing about
E veryone likes them.

Ben Halligan (6)
Duncombe School, Bengeo

My Hero

S upercat is my cat scratching on a mat
U p and away with my hat
P urring a lot on my lap
E njoying a long catnap
R iding down a hill and paying the bill
C urling up annoying Aunt Jill
A cat like that is an amazing cat
T oby my friend has a pet bat!

Libby Mae Sullivan (7)
Duncombe School, Bengeo

My First Acrostic – Little Poets From The South

My Hero

S uper Milly is my cat
U p she goes to get the hat
P ulling herself up onto my lap
E ats lots of grease on the tap
R uns very fast by the cap

M ight be very funny but is very cheeky by the flap
I t is very small but very bright
L ight on its hair
L illy is Milly's friend and she's awake at night
Y eah, Super Milly is here.

Yasmin Jenkins (6)
Duncombe School, Bengeo

Strawberry

S weet and juicy strawberry
T asty and sweet, seedy strawberry
R ough coating to protect the inside
A s red as the reddest fruit in the world
W onderful gleaming coat
B ubbly red bumps
E at it carefully
R ed, scrumptious, luscious strawberry
R ed, scrumptious strawberries
Y ummy strawberry in my tummy.

Harry Sillence (7)
Ellwood Primary School, Ellwood

My First Acrostic - Little Poets From The South

Banana

B ig chunky banana
A s yellow as the sun
N ot as yellow as a lemon
A lways scrumptious
N ot always yellow
A mazing taste.

Hayden Edey (7)
Ellwood Primary School, Ellwood

Grapes

G reen smooth grapes
R ough brown stalk
A nd greener than grass
P ick some lovely grapes
E at lovely, juicy, green grapes
S ome sparkling grapes.

Jack Watkins (7)
Ellwood Primary School, Ellwood

My First Acrostic - Little Poets From The South

Apple

A pples are very scrunchy and yummy

P ulling the apple

P icking apples off the tree

L ove apple

E ating squishy apple.

Chelsea Willetts (6)
Ellwood Primary School, Ellwood

Raspberry

R ed and juicy
A s a lemon
S weet and tasty
P icking beautiful raspberries
B ubbly raspberry
E ating tasty raspberries
R ound raspberry
R osy raspberry
Y ummy raspberry.

Ella Powles (7)
Ellwood Primary School, Ellwood

My First Acrostic - Little Poets From The South

Raspberry

R ed as the reddest thing in the world
A s squashed as a plum
S ofter than a pear
P ears aren't as nice as raspberries
B umpy as gravel
E at raspberries five times a day
R aspberries are very tasty
R aspberry colour
Y ellow is not the colour for a raspberry.

Leon Broom (6)
Ellwood Primary School, Ellwood

Raspberry

R ed and juicy as a pineapple
A s juicy as an apple
S crumptious as a juicy kiwi
P ineapples are not as juicy as raspberries
B ananas are not as yummy as raspberries
E at a raspberry, it is yummy
R ed, squishy raspberries
R ed, juicy, tasty raspberries
Y ummy, lovely raspberries.

Toni Tyler (6)
Ellwood Primary School, Ellwood

Harvest

H elping people is good if you are there for them
A nd if you're there for them you could share your food, be their friend
R aise money for the poor people who have no home and no food
and who are suffering
V icars help us pray for the poor people that we should remember
E ven though you buy food for yourself you could give it
to the poor people at harvest time
S hare your food with the people who are injured
T hank you for harvest Lord!

Cerys Louise Ireland (6)
Finstock CE Primary School, Finstock

Harvest

H elping people every October
A ny people who haven't got food will in October
R ipe fruit is ready to eat
V egetables are ready for you
E at the fruit and vegetables
S hare our food
T he food is ready.

Jack Millard (6)
Finstock CE Primary School, Finstock

Harvest

H elp people and let them have some of your food
we are very lucky to have
A utumn harvest. It is really good if you like to
R aise money for charity. We are
V ery lucky to have harvest festival
E very year if you go to
S chool you should go to harvest festival as well. We should
T hank God for harvest festival.

Barney Foot (6)
Finstock CE Primary School, Finstock

Harvest

H elp people to get blankets
A pples need to be given to people
R un to the church
V icar collects money for the charity
E veryone collects money
S haring
T hank you.

Max (6)
Finstock CE Primary School, Finstock

My First Acrostic – Little Poets From The South

Harvest

H elp people who are poor
A nd give them food and money and clothes
R aise money
V icars are great people
E very harvest is great to help poor people
S uffering people need our help and their health
T hank you for the harvest.

Lizzy Jones (6)
Finstock CE Primary School, Finstock

Harvest

H elp poor people
A nd give them clothes
R aise money to help
V icar is a great person
E very harvest helps
S uffering people need our help
T hank you for harvest.

Lucinda South (6)
Finstock CE Primary School, Finstock

My First Acrostic - Little Poets From The South

Harvest

H elp poor people for new houses
A ll people pray in the church
R aise money for poor people
V egetables can make you strong and fit
E very Tuesday morning everyone who goes to Finstock school prays
S trawberries are good for our harvest
T hank you for all our food and drinks.

Lexi Tipton (6)
Finstock CE Primary School, Finstock

Harvest

H elping people
A utumn
R aise money
V egetables
E veryone eating good food
S haring our food
T hank you for our food.

Lily Holifield, Seth Keats-Hodkinson (6) & Rosie Mullins (5)
Finstock CE Primary School, Finstock

My First Acrostic - Little Poets From The South

Harvest

H elp people in the
A utumn by
R aising money and be
V ery thankful for harvest
E very year
S ome people are very poor. Be very
T hankful for the food we have.

Harriet Howard (5)
Finstock CE Primary School, Finstock

Harvest

H elping
A utumn
R aise money
V egetables
E veryone eating good food
S haring our food
T hank you for our food.

Megan Williams (6)
Finstock CE Primary School, Finstock

Harvest

H orse chestnuts
A corns
R ustling
V ery cloudy
E veryone loves harvest
S unny day
T umbling leaves.

Felicity Marshall (5)
Green Lanes Primary School, Hatfield

Harvest

H arvest leaves are beautiful
A corns
R ed apples
V ery windy
E veryone is happy
S unshine
T ractors.

Aliya Nawaz (5)
Green Lanes Primary School, Hatfield

My First Acrostic - Little Poets From The South

Harvest

H orse chestnuts tumbling
A tumbling leaf
R ustling leaves falling
V ery windy
E veryone likes harvest
S unny day
T umbling.

Iffat Ahmed (6)
Green Lanes Primary School, Hatfield

Harvest

H orses are brown
A corns are brown
R ustling leaves are falling
V ery big haystacks on the farm
E veryone is happy on the farm
S un in the sky
T umbling leaves falling.

Katie Jeffrey (5)
Green Lanes Primary School, Hatfield

My First Acrostic – Little Poets From The South

Harvest

H arvest is coming
A corns are coming
R usting tractor
V ery windy
E very day
S pinning leaves
T urning leaves.

Mia Greenham (6)
Green Lanes Primary School, Hatfield

Harvest

H arvest
A pples falling
R ustling
V ery windy
E verybody likes harvest
S unny
T umbling.

Hannah Paget (5)
Green Lanes Primary School, Hatfield

My First Acrostic - Little Poets From The South

Harvest

H orses galloping
A corn yellow
R ustling red leaves
V ery chilly
E very day acorns are out
S un and rain
T umbling leaves.

Michael Camm (5)
Green Lanes Primary School, Hatfield

Harvest

H orse chestnuts
A corns
R ustling leaves
V ery windy
E verybody is celebrating harvest
S oggy leaves
T ime for harvest.

Matthew Perkins (6)
Green Lanes Primary School, Hatfield

My First Acrostic - Little Poets From The South

Harvest

H appy harvest
A corns brown
R ustling leaves
V ery rainy
E veryone hates rain
S oggy leaves
T wo tractors.

Harry Dobson (6)
Green Lanes Primary School, Hatfield

Harvest

H appy harvest
A corns falling from the trees
R ustling leaves
V ery cloudy
E verybody is celebrating harvest
S carecrow standing in the field
T wisting branches.

Tyana Lister (6)
Green Lanes Primary School, Hatfield

My First Acrostic – Little Poets From The South

Harvest

H orse chestnuts
A busy farmer
R ed apples and green apples
V ery windy day
E verybody is very happy
S weetcorn yellow
T umbling leaves onto the ground.

Katrina Smith (6)
Green Lanes Primary School, Hatfield

Harvest

H orse chestnuts
A pples are green and red
R ustling leaves
V ery sunny
E veryone likes harvest
S unny day
T umbling leaves.

Luke Mann (5)
Green Lanes Primary School, Hatfield

My First Acrostic - Little Poets From The South

Harvest

H orse chestnuts
A yellow leaf
R ustling leaves
V ery windy
E veryone happy
S carecrow
T reasure.

Chloe James (6)
Green Lanes Primary School, Hatfield

Harvest

H appy harvest
A pples tasty
R ustling
V ery windy
E veryone hates rain
S oggy leaves
T wo heavy tractors noisy.

Haylan Dunham (6)
Green Lanes Primary School, Hatfield

My First Acrostic – Little Poets From The South

Harvest

H arvest
A corn is very red
R ustling leaves
V ery rainy
E veryone
S plashing in puddles
T ractor.

Alfie Raynsford (5)
Green Lanes Primary School, Hatfield

Harvest

H arvest is coming
A pples are green
R ustling
V ery rainy
E veryone likes harvest
S carecrow
T ractor.

Holly Toms (6)
Green Lanes Primary School, Hatfield

My First Acrostic – Little Poets From The South

Harvest

H orses can run
A corns
R ustling leaves
V ery big leaves
E veryone likes harvest
S weetcorn
T ractors on the field.

Harry Ballard (5)
Green Lanes Primary School, Hatfield

Harvest

H orse chestnuts
A corns
R ustling
V ery big leaves
E verybody likes leaves
S weetcorn
T ractors on the field.

Ruby Hollywood-Martin (5)
Green Lanes Primary School, Hatfield

My First Acrostic - Little Poets From The South

Flamingo

F laming pink feathers as beautiful as a pink flower
L ong legs as long as a table leg
A mazing small eyes as small as marbles
M ini wings as small as a grown-up's hand
I dle and tired and is also a lovely bird
N osy and lazy, as lazy as an erupting volcano
G rand feathers
O range beak as orange as an orange.

Katie Coan (6)
Green Lanes Primary School, Hatfield

Flamingo

F loppy long legs as long as a piece of string
L arge body
A mazing feathers
M inute eyes
I ncredible eyesight
N early as tall as me
G orgeous bird
O ne lonely flamingo.

Benjamin King (6)
Green Lanes Primary School, Hatfield

My First Acrostic - Little Poets From The South

Flamingo

F unny curly neck
L ong neck, long as an arm
A massive brightness
M ini eyes
I n a very big lake
N early as huge as you
G oing to a river
O ne long pink neck.

Tayla Swaffield (6)
Green Lanes Primary School, Hatfield

Flamingo

F luffy white feathers as white as a blank piece of paper
L ovely pink beak
A mazing tall bird
M ighty small eyes
I like flamingos
N ice flamingo's body
G iant long neck
O ne cool flamingo.

Patrick James Obcena (6)
Green Lanes Primary School, Hatfield

My First Acrostic - Little Poets From The South

Parrot

P retty, light, gloomy, green feathers
A ttractive green and yellow feathers
R ipping show performance
R esisting to try to say, 'Who's a pretty boy?'
O ne of the parrots that can talk any language in the world
T errific birds like the parrot can talk to you
   If you had a parrot you could talk to it.

Matthew Agathangelou (6)
Green Lanes Primary School, Hatfield

Flamingo

F laming pink feathers as beautiful as the sunshine
L egs as big as a chair
A ttractive feathers
M inute, tiny eyes as small as a speck
I nteresting long neck
N early as big as me
G igantic long and bendy neck
O n his own all the time.

Abbie Cook (6)
Green Lanes Primary School, Hatfield

My First Acrostic - Little Poets From The South

Flamingo

F luffy feathers
L ong legs
A tiny eye
M any feathers
I n a lake
N early as tall as me
G reat tail
O range beak.

Molly Hoy (6)
Green Lanes Primary School, Hatfield

Flamingo

F laming face of pink
L ong beak like a volcano exploding
A mazing long legs
M inute, tiny eyes
I ndeed, long legs
N ame is Pimo
G iant feet
O ne flamingo.

Callum Gowing (6)
Green Lanes Primary School, Hatfield

My First Acrostic - Little Poets From The South

Parrot

P retty green feathers
A nice feather
R ed flaming tail
R aising its wings to fly
O n her lovely beak so pretty
T o be as beautiful.

Sophia Monchar (6)
Green Lanes Primary School, Hatfield

Parrot

P retty feathers
A huge beak
R ed feathers
R eally fast to catch its food
O ne lovely parrot
T wo lovely wings.

Zuhayr Mukuddem (6)
Green Lanes Primary School, Hatfield

My First Acrostic - Little Poets From The South

Parrot

P retty beak
A ttractive claws to catch prey
R eally strong wings
R ed tail
O pen big eyes
T alking to us.

Joshua Long (6)
Green Lanes Primary School, Hatfield

Parrot

P retty smooth feathers
A mazing colours like the rainbow
R eally small eyes
R eally loud squawk
O ften flies high
T his bird is beautiful.

Zoe Hunter (6)
Green Lanes Primary School, Hatfield

My First Acrostic - Little Poets From The South

Flamingo

F amous long neck
L azy as an owl
A mazing pink feathers
M ajor, great, pink legs
I nteresting great beak
N atural catching fish
G rand sharp toes
O n it he has somewhere to groom.

Lucian Antippa (7)
Green Lanes Primary School, Hatfield

Parrot

P retty colourful feathers
A ttractive eyes
R ed pretty feathers
R ed flaming tail
O ne good flyer
T iny eyes.

Flower Rosario (6)
Green Lanes Primary School, Hatfield

My First Acrostic - Little Poets From The South

Parrot

P retty parrot
A ttractive feathers
R ed flames
R ed pretty feathers
O ne good parrot
T all as a tree.

Reece Van Genderen (6)
Green Lanes Primary School, Hatfield

Flamingo

F luffy feathers
L ong neck
A mazing long legs
M assive beak
I ndeed, long beak
N early as big as me
G reat tiny eyes
O range beak.

Dana Van Genderen (6)
Green Lanes Primary School, Hatfield

My First Acrostic - Little Poets From The South

Parrot

P retty feathers
A beautiful tail
R ound black eyes
R elaxing near the pond
O n her back
T all as a fat chicken.

Erin Reyner (6)
Green Lanes Primary School, Hatfield

Flamingo

F laming face pink as a rose
L ong, long legs
A mazing beak to catch fish
M inute, small eyes
I nteresting wings
N ever go near
G one in a flash
O ne long neck.

Missie Salmon (6)
Green Lanes Primary School, Hatfield

My First Acrostic – Little Poets From The South

Flamingo

F eathers as pink as a rose
L ying down in the wonderful river
A baby chick comes past her
M ini-eyes as small as a cube
I ncredible legs as long as a tree
N ipping at his food
G racefully walking in the water
O nly one flamingo.

Zainab Jeppe (6)
Green Lanes Primary School, Hatfield

Flamingo

F laming red and pink feathers
L ovely small eyes as small as peas
A mazing wings
M ighty long neck as big as a drainpipe
I like flamingos
N ice beak
G iant legs as big as a ferry
O range feet.

Liam Benson (6)
Green Lanes Primary School, Hatfield

My First Acrostic - Little Poets From The South

Flamingo

F luffy long legs as long as a drainpipe
L arge body as large as three small windows put together
A mazing wings
M inute, tiny eyes
I ncredible head
N ice small beak
G iant long neck
O ne big flamingo.

Joshua Paul (7)
Green Lanes Primary School, Hatfield

Flamingo

F luffy long neck as long as a snake sticking his enormous tongue out
L ovely burnt orange legs with toes as sharp as spikes
A mazing wings that are as light as a fairy
M inute, tiny eyes as small as an ant
I ncredible flying through the deep, sea-blue sky
N apping in the lovely tree
G reat bird flying through the lovely sky
O ften flies very. very high to the bright golden sun.

James Mann (6)
Green Lanes Primary School, Hatfield

Flamingo

F luffy feathers
L ong legs
A ttractive feathers
M assive eyes
I nteresting feathers
N early as tall as me
G iant feet
O range beak.

Eve Betteridge (6)
Green Lanes Primary School, Hatfield

Harvest

H arvest is great
A corns are falling
R ustling leaves
V ery windy
E veryone likes harvest
S carecrows are scaring the crows away
T rees are tall.

Gemma Cutbill (5)
Green Lanes Primary School, Hatfield

Eco

E co school
C heerful children
O ften.

Katie Leefarr (6)
Howe Dell Primary School, Hatfield

Howe Dell

H elping other people
O pen to everyone
W ins competitions
E co school

D ustbin
E co desks
L ots of fun
L ots of learning.

Freddie Houlahan (6)
Howe Dell Primary School, Hatfield

My First Acrostic - Little Poets From The South

Eco

E co school
C ollect rubbish
O pen to everyone.

Shaun Michael Shoda (6)
Howe Dell Primary School, Hatfield

Eco Squad

- E co school
- C lean classroom
- O utdoor class

- S olar panels
- Q uiet lunchtime
- U nbelievable climbing frame
- A lovely school
- D oors.

Jodie Garg (6)
Howe Dell Primary School, Hatfield

My First Acrostic – Little Poets From The South

Howe Dell

H ungry
O range
W ork
E co squad

D on't mess
E co school
L earning
L iteracy.

Bailey Quinn (6)
Howe Dell Primary School, Hatfield

Howe Dell

H oles in the wall
O pen
W ooden climbing frame
E co school

D oors open for you
E co squad
L earning
L istening.

Stephanie Raine (6)
Howe Dell Primary School, Hatfield

My First Acrostic - Little Poets From The South

Eco

E co squad
C limbing frame
O utdoor classroom.

Harry-Tom Brinkley (6)
Howe Dell Primary School, Hatfield

Howe Dell

H elp everyone
O pen
W e listen to the teachers
E veryone is eco

D o what the teacher says
E veryone is kind
L ove our school
L ook after our school.

Ayo Ajayi (6)
Howe Dell Primary School, Hatfield

My First Acrostic - Little Poets From The South

Howe Dell

H owe Dell
O utdoor classroom
W ind turbine
E co school

D elightful teachers
E co squad
L earning
L istening.

Emma Roberts (6)
Howe Dell Primary School, Hatfield

Eco Squad

E co
C ool
O pen

S chool
Q uiet
U nderstanding the world
A mazing
D on't be naughty.

Tanvi Sofat (6)
Howe Dell Primary School, Hatfield

My First Acrostic - Little Poets From The South

Howe Dell

H appy
O pen
W ind turbine
E co school

D ustbins
E co squad
L aughing
L earning.

Sophia Kleovoulou (6)
Howe Dell Primary School, Hatfield

Eco

E co squad
C ool school
O h what a wonderful school.

Kiera Chapman (6)
Howe Dell Primary School, Hatfield

My First Acrostic – Little Poets From The South

Howe Dell

H appy school
O pen for business
W onder days
E co warrior

D elivered fruit
E lectricity
L ighting is powered
L essons are fun.

Scarlett Brown (6)
Howe Dell Primary School, Hatfield

Howe Dell

H elpful teachers
O pportunities
W ind turbine
E nvironmentally friendly

D rama is rich
E xciting learning
L ights are powered by sun
L aughter.

Camryn Whitney (6)
Howe Dell Primary School, Hatfield

My First Acrostic - Little Poets From The South

Howe Dell

H unger, lunch at school
O ctober at school
W e're all here I think
E co school we are

D ays are good
E lectronic lights
L iteracy is fun, I love it
L ove the school.

Georgia Stratton (6)
Howe Dell Primary School, Hatfield

Howe Dell

H appy
O pen all year
W onderful
E co

D elicious dinner
E xcellent
L ovely school
L ovely people.

Mia Ross (7)
Howe Dell Primary School, Hatfield

My First Acrostic - Little Poets From The South

Howe Dell

H owe Dell
O ut of this world
W ind turbine
E xcellent

D elicious food
E co
L ovely
L ovely.

Trystan Sam-Fat (6)
Howe Dell Primary School, Hatfield

Rene

R iding horses is my favourite thing
E ats sausages
N ice for my brother
E njoys parties.

Rene Burke (6)
Longcot & Fernham Primary School, Longcot

My First Acrostic - Little Poets From The South

Katie

K atie is my name
A cat and dog are my favourite
T ries hard in her work
I like sausages with my dinner
E ating is my favourite.

Katie Griffin (5)
Longcot & Fernham Primary School, Longcot

Max

M ax is very great
A dding is great fun
X -rays are scary, they feel funny

W hitfield is my second name
H air is so beautiful
I like the colour red
T homas is my middle name
F ields I like to play in
I like going on the beach
E ars help me listen to music
L ewis is my friend
D ad is the best.

Max Whitfield (7)
Longcot & Fernham Primary School, Longcot

My First Acrostic – Little Poets From The South

Fireworks

F abulous fireworks glittering
I n the sky
R ainbow colours
E xplode everywhere
W histling and banging
O range, yellow, blue, purple and pink
R ockets zooming
K eeping warm under the stars
S parkle and twinkle, that's what fireworks do.

Daisy Harvey (6)
Maple Cross JMI & Nursery School, Maple Cross

Family

F amily means no one gets forgotten
A nd we love each other
M y family never gets left out
I love my family
L ots of people in my family
Y ou have got a family.

Charlotte Hatswell (6)
Maple Cross JMI & Nursery School, Maple Cross

My First Acrostic - Little Poets From The South

Winter Is Here

W histling cold winds blow through my hair
I ce and snow is everywhere
N oses are all red
T rees are bare with no leaves to wear
E veryone is singing a Christmas song
R obins love bobbing along.

Bradley Holloway (6)
Maple Cross JMI & Nursery School, Maple Cross

Trees Acrostic

T rees are dying
R ed, brown and orange
E very leaf is tumbling down
E lm, oak, ash and beech
S oon the trees are bare.

Alexandra Maggs (6)
Meldreth Primary School, Meldreth

My First Acrostic - Little Poets From The South

Autumn Acrostic

A utumn leaves fall from the trees
U gly leaves crunch on the trees
T he conkers fall from trees
U mbrellas go up and down
M agic and colourful, pretty leaves
N uts, nuts good for you!

Amelia Close (6)
Meldreth Primary School, Meldreth

Autumn Acrostic

A pples fall and die
U mbrellas go up
T he wind is whistling
U p goes the smoke
M ornings are cold
N ights are dark.

Aoife Brophy (6)
Meldreth Primary School, Meldreth

Trees Acrostic

T he leaves of trees are tumbling down
R otten leaves lying on the ground
E very day more and more
E very hour conkers fall
S oon the trees are bare.

Conall Fergus (6)
Meldreth Primary School, Meldreth

Autumn Acrostic

A utumn is fun
U p goes the smoke
T he leaves are yellow, red
U p goes a squirrel
M any leaves fall down
N ights are dark.

Elisha Plester (6)
Meldreth Primary School, Meldreth

Trees Acrostic

T rees losing leaves
R ustling nests falling from trees
E very day leaves are twirling
E lm, ash, oak and beech
S un shining in the sky.

Erin Fergus (6)
Meldreth Primary School, Meldreth

Autumn Acrostic

A corns are cracking off the trees
U gly trees when they have no leaves
T wisting, tumbling leaves in autumn
U gly brown leaves twisting off the trees
M ornings are freezing cold
N aughty leaves are falling on me.

Leila Kermani (6)
Meldreth Primary School, Meldreth

My First Acrostic - Little Poets From The South

Autumn Acrostic

A corns dropping from trees
U gly leaves falling down
T rees changing colour
U nusual coloured skies
M agical, floating, flying
N uts buried from squirrels.

Morgan Robson (6)
Meldreth Primary School, Meldreth

Leaf Acrostic

L eaves falling
E very day
A corns on your head
F inding nuts.

Shannon Casling (6)
Meldreth Primary School, Meldreth

My First Acrostic - Little Poets From The South

Autumn Acrostic

A utumn days are brilliant
U gly leaves when they turn all brown
T rees lose their leaves
U gly leaves turn browny-green
M isty days in autumn
N o leaves are on me.

Tia Misgrove (6)
Meldreth Primary School, Meldreth

Baby Sam

B aby Sam is a baby full of fun
A nd he loves his food
B ut, oh dear, what a mess
Y ou should see Sam

S ometimes he flaps his arms
A nd we think he's trying to fly
M y baby brother Sam.

Joshua Sibley (7)
Minchinhampton Primary School, Minchinhampton

Chocolate

C hocolate's yummy and
H ot, I warm it
O n a campfire
C ooking and stirring
O n a starry night
L ovely with marshmallows in
A nd I'm sleepy now
T ime to go to bed at the
E nd of the day.

Grace Southgate (6)
Minchinhampton Primary School, Minchinhampton

Swimming

S plashing around in the water
W ishing to be like a mermaid
I want to swim like a fish
M aybe I might get to the Olympics or
M aybe I might get to gold
I f I get to the Olympics I want to win
N ext I might
G o to gymnastics!

Jenny Weir (6)
Minchinhampton Primary School, Minchinhampton

My First Acrostic - Little Poets From The South

My Harvest Poem

H arvest time is here
A pples, nice and juicy
R ipe plums, ready to be picked and ready to be eaten
V egetables nice and crunchy
E verybody celebrates the harvest
S hare the harvest
T hank you God for fruit and vegetables.

Holly Rebecca Hamblin (6)
Minchinhampton Primary School, Minchinhampton

Ben Ten

B lasting through the air
E ven the Omnitrix cannot destroy
N ew and strong, leader of Ben

T oad that was giant and poisonous
E ventually Ben slammed his watch
N ow that enemy is destroyed.

Ronan Lynch (6)
Minchinhampton Primary School, Minchinhampton

My First Acrostic - Little Poets From The South

Amy Miller

A lways sensible
M usical
Y ounger sister

M akes funny jokes
I nteresting
L ikes the colour yellow
L istens carefully
E njoys writing
R eads stories.

Amy Miller (6)
St Hilda's School, Harpenden

Becky Walter

B rilliant
E xcellent
C areful
K ind and likes
Y ellow

W atches X Factor
A mazing
L ikes lavender and
T hrushes
E njoys work
R eads a lot.

Becky Walter (6)
St Hilda's School, Harpenden

Tilly

T houghtful
I nterested in art
L ikes ice cream
L oves flowers and
Y ellow clothes.

Tilly Johnstone (6)
St Hilda's School, Harpenden

Madeline

M agnificent
A lways very lively
D oes a lot of smiling
E njoys going on long trips
L oves eating Chinese takeaways
I nterested in animals and
N ature
E ven adopted a polar bear.

Madeline Pritchard (6)
St Hilda's School, Harpenden

My First Acrostic - Little Poets From The South

Lottie Bentall

L ovely
O ften giggly
T idy
T ries hard
I nterested in frogs
E xceptionally amusing

B rilliant at maths
E njoys school
N eat
T houghtful
A nimal lover
L istens
L ikes animals.

Lottie Bentall (6)
St Hilda's School, Harpenden

Annabel Davis

A lways good
N ever naughty
N ever scribbles
A musing
B rilliant
E njoys maths
L ikes English and

D iving
A mazing
V ery funny
I nterested in geography and
S cience.

Annabel Davis (6)
St Hilda's School, Harpenden

My First Acrostic - Little Poets From The South

Eve Graham

E xcited
V ery cheerful
E ats sweets

G rowing
R eads stories
A mazing
H appy
A dores puppies
M akes cakes.

Eve Graham (6)
St Hilda's School, Harpenden

Maddie Desmond

M y favourite colour is blue
A nimal lover
D reams about Snoopy
D oesn't like maths
I nterested in 'Hello Kitty'
E njoys lunch

D oes gym
E ach day I have fun
S cared of the dark
M y dogs are cute
O ften makes cakes
N ever watch football
D on't like science.

Maddie Desmond (6)
St Hilda's School, Harpenden

My First Acrostic - Little Poets From The South

Charlotte

C hocolate lover
H orses
A dventures in the garden
R eading
L ikes ice cream
O ften go on the
T rampoline, play
T ennis
E njoy going to the park.

Charlotte Gibson (6)
St Hilda's School, Harpenden

Hannah Ritchie

H elpful
A dventurous
N ice
N oisy
A ctive
H appy

R emembers things
I nterested
T ries hard
C heeky
H orse lover
I ce cream eater
E xcellent.

Hannah Ritchie (6)
St Hilda's School, Harpenden

My First Acrostic - Little Poets From The South

Ella

E njoyable person
L oves laughing
L ively
A nimal lover.

Ella Murphy (6)
St Hilda's School, Harpenden

Rosaleen

R eading books
O pens the door for people
S weets are my favourite
A lways asking
L ikes school
E ats pizza
E lla is my best friend
N ice to people.

Rosaleen Mackie (6)
St Hilda's School, Harpenden

Matthew

M unching my food
A pples are my favourite, but only half
T rains are my favourite toys
T homas the Tank is fun
H orses are my mum's favourite
E ggs boiled for breakfast - lovely
W ater is good when you're thirsty.

Matthew Kinnersley (6)
Sibford Junior School, Sibford Ferris

Elena

E ggs are horrible
L ollipops are my favourite sweet
E very day I go to school
N o carrots in my fridge
A pples are my best fruit!

Elena Swift (5)
Sibford Junior School, Sibford Ferris

My First Acrostic - Little Poets From The South

Oliver

O ranges are my favourite food
L ove the bike in my playground
I love my mummy
V ery cheeky my friend is
E very X Factor is my best show
R obin is our school cleaner.

Oliver Meadows (6)
Sibford Junior School, Sibford Ferris

Sam

S inging 'Ting-a-lay-o'!
A t school
M y jumper is made of wool.

Sam Jervis (5)
Sibford Junior School, Sibford Ferris

My First Acrostic - Little Poets From The South

Sammy

S paghetti is my favourite food
A pples are juicy
M y mum is kind
M y dad has a speedboat
Y ou are my favourite teacher.

Sammy Vintcent (5)
Sibford Junior School, Sibford Ferris

Seaside

S unny
E ating ice cream
A ngry waves
S lippy seaweed
I cy water
D rinking apple juice
E xcited children.

Connor Lightfoot
Trotts Hill Primary School, Stevenage

My First Acrostic - Little Poets From The South

Seaside

S lippery seaweed
E xtreme heat
A mazing crabs
S hiny sand
I ncredible dolphins
D elicious ice cream
E normous waves.

Kieran Lawrence (6)
Trotts Hill Primary School, Stevenage

Seaside

S hining shells hiding in the sand
E xcited children waiting to get an ice cream
A mazing sandcastles, glittering in the sun
S hips sailing on the blue sea
I cy ice creams melting in the sun
D elightful dolphins, splashing in the sea
E xciting helter-skelter on the beach.

Zoe Booyse (6)
Trotts Hill Primary School, Stevenage

My First Acrostic - Little Poets From The South

Seaside

S and is glittery
E ating delicious ice cream
A ngry waves
S ome delicious chops to eat
I mperfect sandcastles
D rinking juice
E xcited children playing on the sand.

Brandon Cowen (6)
Trotts Hill Primary School, Stevenage

Seaside

S hining blue sea, sliding onto the sand
E xcited children playing in the sea
A mazing shells, sparkling in the sand
S parkling sand on the beach
I ce cold seas slipping onto the sand
D olphins splashing in the sea
E veryone is eating ice cream.

Hannah Field (6)
Trotts Hill Primary School, Stevenage

My First Acrostic - Little Poets From The South

Seaside

S queaking seals making a lot of noise
E xcited children grabbing a bucket and spade
A mazing dolphins splashing in the waves
S lippery rocks sliding away from me
I ncredible waves crashing on the rocks
D elicious, scrumptious ice cream
E veryone has energy for running about in the deep blue sea.

Darcée Norton (7)
Trotts Hill Primary School, Stevenage

Seaside

S eagulls squawking and flying in the air
E ating gorgeous flavoured ice cream
A mazing dolphins pouncing out of the glittery sea
S hips sailing on the sea and waves
I ncredible, enormous, yellow sandcastles
D elightful dolphins jumping with their pod
E xhausted people lying on rugs.

Siân Yvonne Worton (6)
Trotts Hill Primary School, Stevenage

My First Acrostic - Little Poets From The South

Seaside

S eagulls squeaking on an enormous rock on the beach
E ating delicious strawberry ice cream with a red cherry on top
A mazing dolphins splashing in the silvery-blue sea
S hining patterns on pretty shells
I nteresting fish swimming in the blue sea with their family
D elightful dolphins jumping in the shining blue sea
E xcited crabs, snip-snapping in the sea.

Caitlin Hood (6)
Trotts Hill Primary School, Stevenage

Seaside

S eagulls are flying around the seaside
E xcited children running to the ice cream van
A mazing dolphins are on the waves
S hining sun in the sky
I cy ice cream cooling me down
D irty sand on my hand
E normous seaside, where I have fun.

Bilal Ahmed (7)
Trotts Hill Primary School, Stevenage

My First Acrostic - Little Poets From The South

Seaside

S un shining down on my skin
E ating delicious ice cream, trying all of the flavours with a cherry on top
A mazing children playing on the beach
S hop on the beach selling ice cream and candyfloss
I am at the beach with Harry and Jack in the cold sea
D elicious mint ice cream with a flake on top
E normous waves crashing all around.

Quincy Hayward Provencal (7)
Trotts Hill Primary School, Stevenage

Seaside

S creeching seagulls flying around
E normous waves all around
A good day at the beach
S corching hot sunshine
I ce cream is melting
D elicious chips to eat
E veryone is happy at the beach.

Megan Wilkins (6)
Trotts Hill Primary School, Stevenage

My First Acrostic - Little Poets From The South

Things I Like

G ardening, giraffes
E lephants, eggs
M agic, marmalade
M onkeys, masks
A pples and peas.

Gemma Hemmings (5)
Trotts Hill Primary School, Stevenage

Things I Like

S wimming skeletons
H opping hens
A ngry apples
N aughty nuts
E ating elephants.

Shane Clynes (5)
Trotts Hill Primary School, Stevenage

My First Acrostic - Little Poets From The South

Things I Like

A pples, animals
L ollipops, lighthouses
E agles, eggs
X -rays, xylophones.

Alex McCarthy (5)
Trotts Hill Primary School, Stevenage

Things I Like

K angaroos kissing
I ce cream, insects
M onkeys and money
B lue, bananas
E agles' eggs
R ed roses
L ambs, leaves
E lephants eating
Y ellow yo-yo.

Kimberley Glander (5)
Trotts Hill Primary School, Stevenage

My First Acrostic - Little Poets From The South

Things I Like

R abbits, rainbows
E lephants, eagles, eggs
B lue, butterflies
E aster eggs
C hocolate, computers
C obwebs, crackers
A pples, alligators.

Rebecca Honeysett (5)
Trotts Hill Primary School, Stevenage

Things I Like

A pples, ants
L ollipops, lions
I ce cream, insects
C aps, cats
I nstruments, ink
A ntelopes, acting.

Alicia Bachelor (5)
Trotts Hill Primary School, Stevenage

My First Acrostic - Little Poets From The South

Things I Like

C abbage, cars
A pples, aeroplanes
I ce skating
T en teddies
L icking lollies
I roning
N ice noodles.

Caitlin Redmond (5)
Trotts Hill Primary School, Stevenage

Things I Like

A mbulances, apples
B ananas, boys
I roning, insects
G uitars, garages
A irports, ants
I cy ice
L ovely lions.

Abigail Craig (5)
Trotts Hill Primary School, Stevenage

My First Acrostic - Little Poets From The South

Things I Like

C licking camel
H opping hare
A cting ant
R unning rabbit
L icking lion
I cy iguana
E xciting elephants.

Charlie Andrews (5)
Trotts Hill Primary School, Stevenage

Things I Like

C ats, cake
H amsters, hats
A pples, ants
R ainbows, rain
L ollipops, lemons
I nsects, ice cream
E elephants, eggs.

Charlie Cameron (5)
Trotts Hill Primary School, Stevenage

My First Acrostic - Little Poets From The South

Things I Like

O range, owls
L emon, lambs
I cicle, ice cream
V ases, videos
I ce, igloos
A nts, alligators.

Olivia O'Sullivan (5)
Trotts Hill Primary School, Stevenage

Things I Like

P laying, parties
E lephants, eating
M onkeys, money
B uns, bears
E ggs, eagles.

Pembe Pekoz (5)
Trotts Hill Primary School, Stevenage

My First Acrostic - Little Poets From The South

Things I Like

J am, jeans, jumping
A nts, apples
C ars, cats
K angaroos, kittens.

Jack Mitchell (5)
Trotts Hill Primary School, Stevenage

Things I Like

O ctopus, orange
L ollipops, ladybirds
I gloos, insects
V olcanoes, vegetables
E lephants, eggs
R abbits, rhinos.

Oliver Crake (5)
Trotts Hill Primary School, Stevenage

My First Acrostic – Little Poets From The South

Things I Like

Grapes, guitars
Elephants, eggs
Octopus, oranges
Rabbits, running
Gardening
Eating, eagles.

George Ashby (5)
Trotts Hill Primary School, Stevenage

Things I Like

R eading, running
E ggs, eagles
E lephants, eating
C oins, cats
E mpty engines.

Reece Sullivan (5)
Trotts Hill Primary School, Stevenage

My First Acrostic - Little Poets From The South

Things I Like

H amsters, helicopters
U pside-down umbrellas
A pples, airports
N ests, nuts.

Huan Xu (5)
Trotts Hill Primary School, Stevenage

Things I Like

L icking lollies
E lephants
O ctopus.

Leo Ferrari (5)
Trotts Hill Primary School, Stevenage

My First Acrostic - Little Poets From The South

Things I Like

C ross cats
A ngry ants
M ice, monkeys
E ating, elephants
R unning robbers
O range octopus
N aughty nuts.

Cameron King (5)
Trotts Hill Primary School, Stevenage

Things I Like

O ctopus, ostrich
L ego, lion
I nsect, igloos
V ans, vines
E ggs, elephants
R ockets, robots.

Oliver Wright (6)
Trotts Hill Primary School, Stevenage

My First Acrostic - Little Poets From The South

Jodie

J ade is my sister
O livia is my friend
D olphins are my favourite animals
I am lovely
E llie is my sister.

Jodie (5)
Wheatcroft Primary School, Hertford

Elise

E veryone is my friend
L ovely and nice I am
I like myself
S miley
E lise is my name.

Elise Ainge (5)
Wheatcroft Primary School, Hertford

My First Acrostic - Little Poets From The South

Horses

Helping horse galloping by saying, 'Hi!'
Out the barn she goes galloping
Riding. People on her back
Singing and dancing she goes with her toes
Every day she gets to run out in the sun
Step by step she goes to her barn for bed.

Chloe Carter (6)
Wheatcroft Primary School, Hertford

Panda

P retty, little, cute panda
A nxious little panda
N aughty, cuddly panda
D arling, little, fluffy panda
A ngry, little, soft panda.

Lara Craig (6)
Wheatcroft Primary School, Hertford

My First Acrostic – Little Poets From The South

Lion

L eaping lion
I ntelligent animal
O n the hunt for other animals
N o one knows they are prowling by.

Alastair Murray (7)
Wheatcroft Primary School, Hertford

Panda

P andas eat bamboo. They like it
A panda has a black and white body
N ice pandas climb up trees and
D rink out of a river
A panda lives in a forest.

Rebecca Collins (6)
Wheatcroft Primary School, Hertford

My First Acrostic - Little Poets From The South

Tiger

T he tiger is strong
I n his mouth he has sharp teeth
G reat, big, stripy tiger
E veryone is scared of his pointy ears
R oar, roar, roar. That's how the tiger goes.

Elizabeth Appleford (6)
Wheatcroft Primary School, Hertford

Panda

P retty panda, black and white
A panda eats bamboo
N ot one is alive
D on't kill pandas
A lways like to climb trees.

Kieran Paxton (6)
Wheatcroft Primary School, Hertford

My First Acrostic - Little Poets From The South

Rabbits

R abbits are rough and shy
A bouncy rabbit has floppy ears
B ouncing up and down, underground they dig
B iting people with their teeth
I 'd like one for a pet
T hey are very cute, rabbits are.

Sophie Pratt (6)
Wheatcroft Primary School, Hertford

Horses

H orses have hard hooves
O ut the barn she goes to eat
R acing proudly round the field
S ilently and shyly sitting down
E veryone says horses are cute and cuddly
S ome people say they're beautiful and friendly.

Leanna Rhodes (6)
Wheatcroft Primary School, Hertford

My First Acrostic - Little Poets From The South

Elephant

E normous elephant stomping through the forest
L azy elephants sleeping
E ating lots of food
P retty elephant dancing
H appy elephant stomping
A dventurous elephant
N aughty elephant stomping
T iny elephant walking.

Toby Hill (6)
Wheatcroft Primary School, Hertford

Enormous

E normous elephant stomping
L azy elephant snoozing
E xciting elephant
P rancing elephant
H appy elephant, smiling
A ngry elephant
N aughty elephant
T idy elephant.

Hester Peart (5)
Wheatcroft Primary School, Hertford

Black Bear

B lack bear, asleep in the rain
E veryone is scared
A wake, he roars
R unning away!

James Welch (5)
Wheatcroft Primary School, Hertford

Young Writers Information

We hope you have enjoyed reading this book - and that you will continue to enjoy it in the coming years.

If you like reading and writing poetry drop us a line, or give us a call, and we'll send you a free information pack.

Alternatively if you would like to order further copies of this book or any of our other titles, then please give us a call or log onto our website at www.youngwriters.co.uk.

Young Writers Information
Remus House
Coltsfoot Drive
Peterborough
PE2 9JX
(01733) 890066